#JUSTMYTHOUGHTS

THE INTRO:

I Use
To Give My
POWER Away,

. . .

Yet Goodness
of "The Divine"
Proceeds With
"Feminine" GRACE;
Therefore,
I COMMAND MY SHIFT!

. . .

Novah's Son

#JUSTMYTHOUGHTS

STEP INTO YOUR ABUNDANCE:

WISDOM:

WELL KNOWN KNOWLEDGE OF WHAT YOU'RE HEALING, LEARNING AND EVOLVING FROM.

HEALING:

ENTER INTO A STATE OF TRANSMUTATION AND TRANSFORMATION INSIDE OUT. HEALING THOUGHTS, WORDS, ACTIONS AND ESSENCE INTO THE REALITY AS WELL AS THE SPIRIT OF LIFE.

WEALTH:

MENTALLY ALIGN AND EMOTIONALLY EMBRACE THE VIBRATION OF PURE FULFILLMENT WITHIN THE HEART OF WISDOM AS GRATITUDE & PEACE. EXPERIENCE YOUR PROSPERITY.

ABUNDANCE:

BRINGING IN THE RICHES OF UNIVERSAL FAVOR THROUGH SPIRITUAL, VIBRATIONAL & MATERIAL NOTIONS.

HOW DO YOU CREATE & ATTRACT

ABUNDANCE

IN YOUR LIFE?!

Manifest The Life You Don't Need A Vacation From:

CREATE YOUR HAPPINESS:

Be ENCHANTING.
ENVISION What You See For Yourself.
VIBRATE With Gratitude.

_____
_____
_____
_____
_____
_____
_____
_____
_____
_____
_____

DATE: MANIFESTATION GOAL:

I'M GRATEFUL FOR: ONE STEP @ A TIME:

Manifest The Life You Don't Need A Vacation From:

CREATE YOUR HAPPINESS:

Be ENCHANTING.
ENVISION What You See For Yourself.
VIBRATE With Gratitude.

_____

_____

_____

_____

_____

_____

_____

_____

_____

_____

_____

_____

_____

_____

_____

I BOUGHT
THE DAMN CAKE

FOR YOU TO ENJOY

I'M FAR FROM MAD,
YOU STARTED EATING!

.   .   .

I JUST NOTICED
HOW BEGAN TO MISTREAT ME,

KNOWING

I'VE BEEN FEEDING YOU!

#NOWLICKMYMIDDLEFINGERCLEAN

Call Your POWER Back!

Manifest The Life You Don't Need A Vacation From:

CREATE YOUR HAPPINESS:

Be ENCHANTING.
ENVISION What You See For Yourself.
VIBRATE With Gratitude.

_____

_____

_____

_____

_____

_____

_____

_____

_____

_____

_____

DATE: MANIFESTATION GOAL:

I'M GRATEFUL FOR: ONE STEP @ A TIME:

Manifest The Life You Don't Need A Vacation From:

Be ENCHANTING.
ENVISION What You See For Yourself.
VIBRATE With Gratitude.

_____

_____

_____

_____

_____

_____

_____

_____

_____

_____

_____

_____

_____

_____

_____

_____

_____

#JUSTMYTHOUGHTS

PEACE

IS WHEN TIME DOESN'T MATTER AS IT PASSES BY

...

- MARIA SCHELL

Surrender To Your Mission.

Manifest The Life You Don't Need A Vacation From:

CREATE YOUR HAPPINESS:

Be ENCHANTING.
ENVISION What You See For Yourself.
VIBRATE With Gratitude.

_____

_____

_____

_____

_____

_____

_____

_____

_____

_____

_____

_____

DATE: MANIFESTATION GOAL:

I'M GRATEFUL FOR: ONE STEP @ A TIME:

Manifest The Life You Don't Need A Vacation From:

CREATE YOUR HAPPINESS:

Be ENCHANTING.
ENVISION What You See For Yourself.
VIBRATE With Gratitude.

_____

_____

_____

_____

_____

_____

_____

_____

_____

_____

_____

_____

_____

_____

_____

_____

_____

_____

#JUSTMYTHOUGHTS

YES!
SOMETIMES ... JUST SOMETIMES
THE EVENTS OF LIFE
WILL KNOCK YOU ON YOUR ASS.

YET,
–

IT'S YOUR MISSION,

TO GET UP!

–

AS HAPPINESS,
ISN'T THE ABSENCE OF WAR.
NOR TROUBLES. NOR ISSUES.
NOR DRAMA. NOR OBSTACLES.
. . .
YET THE ABILITY
TO EMBRACE TRUST
IN YOUR OWN
RIGHTS.
WRONGS.
WILLINGNESS.
&
DECISIONS
TO HANDLE THEM
ACCORDINGLY!

Trust The Process!

Manifest The Life You Don't Need A Vacation From:

CREATE YOUR HAPPINESS:

Be ENCHANTING.
ENVISION What You See For Yourself.
VIBRATE With Gratitude.

_____

_____

_____

_____

_____

_____

_____

_____

_____

_____

_____

DATE: MANIFESTATION GOAL:

I'M GRATEFUL FOR: ONE STEP @ A TIME:

Manifest The Life You Don't Need A Vacation From:

CREATE YOUR HAPPINESS:

Be ENCHANTING.
ENVISION What You See For Yourself.
VIBRATE With Gratitude.

_____

_____

_____

_____

_____

_____

_____

_____

_____

_____

_____

_____

_____

_____

_____

_____

#JUSTMYTHOUGHTS

OTHER
PEOPLE'S

SENSE
DO
NOT
ADD
UP
WHEN
YOU
ARE

-

PRICELESS!

Divine & Align.

Manifest The Life You Don't Need A Vacation From:

Be ENCHANTING.
ENVISION What You See For Yourself.
VIBRATE With Gratitude.

_____

_____

_____

_____

_____

_____

_____

_____

_____

_____

_____

DATE: MANIFESTATION GOAL:

I'M GRATEFUL FOR: ONE STEP @ A TIME:

Manifest The Life You Don't Need A Vacation From:

CREATE YOUR HAPPINESS:

Be ENCHANTING.
ENVISION What You See For Yourself.
VIBRATE With Gratitude.

_____

_____

_____

_____

_____

_____

_____

_____

_____

_____

_____

_____

_____

_____

_____

_____

_____

_____

IS IT
REALLY
IN DIVINE
BETTERMENT
TO TAKE WHAT
DOES NOT BELONG
TO YOU THAN TO LET IT
LIE AROUND NEGLECTED!?

Take Action When Guided.

Manifest The Life You Don't Need A Vacation From:

CREATE YOUR HAPPINESS:

Be ENCHANTING.
ENVISION What You See For Yourself.
VIBRATE With Gratitude.

_____
_____
_____
_____
_____
_____
_____
_____
_____
_____
_____
_____

DATE: MANIFESTATION GOAL:

I'M GRATEFUL FOR: ONE STEP @ A TIME:

Manifest The Life You Don't Need A Vacation From:

CREATE YOUR HAPPINESS:

Be ENCHANTING.
ENVISION What You See For Yourself.
VIBRATE With Gratitude.

_____

_____

_____

_____

_____

_____

_____

_____

_____

_____

_____

_____

_____

_____

_____

_____

_____

#JUSTMYTHOUGHTS

IN
HISTORY,
—
WE ACCESS
KNOWLEDGE.

TO
REPEAT WITH
NO FOUNDATION,
NO UNDERSTANDING,
NO PURPOSE,
NO TRANSMUTATION,
NO GROWTH,
NO TRANSFORAMTION;
—
DELAYS THE
EVOLUTION OF
WISDOM.

Experience Is Wisdom.

Manifest The Life You Don't Need A Vacation From:

CREATE YOUR HAPPINESS:

Be ENCHANTING.
ENVISION What You See For Yourself.
VIBRATE With Gratitude.

_____
_____
_____
_____
_____
_____
_____
_____
_____
_____
_____
_____

DATE: MANIFESTATION GOAL:

I'M GRATEFUL FOR: ONE STEP @ A TIME:

Manifest The Life You Don't Need A Vacation From:

CREATE YOUR HAPPINESS:

Be ENCHANTING.
ENVISION What You See For Yourself.
VIBRATE With Gratitude.

#JUSTMYTHOUGHTS

THE MOMENT YOUR PHONE
BEGINS TO VIBRATE
WHILE IN YOUR LAP
& YOU HESITATE
TO ANSWER

. . .

JUST TO LET
IT MARINATE
FOR 2.5, LOL
"NEW PHONE WHO DIS"?!
IT DOESN'T REALLY
MATTER DOES IT??
DON'T GOTTA PICK UP
RIGHT AWAY HUH?!

- - - - - -

TUH, I BET

#SelfCare Is A Must!

Manifest The Life You Don't Need A Vacation From:

CREATE YOUR HAPPINESS:

Be ENCHANTING.
ENVISION What You See For Yourself.
VIBRATE With Gratitude.

_____

_____

_____

_____

_____

_____

_____

_____

_____

_____

_____

DATE: MANIFESTATION GOAL:

I'M GRATEFUL FOR: ONE STEP @ A TIME:

Manifest The Life You Don't Need A Vacation From:

CREATE YOUR HAPPINESS:

Be ENCHANTING.
ENVISION What You See For Yourself.
VIBRATE With Gratitude.

_____

_____

_____

_____

_____

_____

_____

_____

_____

_____

_____

_____

_____

_____

#JUSTMYTHOUGHTS

SOME OF THE DOPEST:
-
PARTIES
GET TOGETHERS
NIGHT CLUBS
STRIP CLUBS
GAME NIGHTS
LADIES NIGHT
BBQS

WHATEVER THE
CELEBRATION
OR FUNCTION
I'VE BEEN TO
. . .
GOES DOWN
IN MY HEAD!

#IT'SLIT

Ritual With Consistency!

Manifest The Life You Don't Need A Vacation From:

Be ENCHANTING.
ENVISION What You See For Yourself.
VIBRATE With Gratitude.

_____

_____

_____

_____

_____

_____

_____

_____

_____

_____

_____

_____

DATE: MANIFESTATION GOAL:

I'M GRATEFUL FOR: ONE STEP @ A TIME:

Manifest The Life You Don't Need A Vacation From:

CREATE YOUR HAPPINESS:

Be ENCHANTING.
ENVISION What You See For Yourself.
VIBRATE With Gratitude.

SEE YOUR VOICE,
IN SPIRIT!

–

IT'S NOT ALWAYS ABOUT:

SCREAMING TO BE HEARD.
YELLING TO SPEAK TO YOUR MIND.
CUSSING TO DEPICT YOUR THOUGHTS.
BELITTLING WITH NAME CALLING.
SHOWING OFF AS IF YOU'RE "JUST" JOKING.
ANNOUNCING IT TO SOCIAL MEDIA.

–

IF THE MESSAGE CAN OPEN DOORS,
REMEMBER DELIVERY IS KEY.

–

YES! YOUR POINT IS VALID.
YES! THEY SEE YOU.
YES! YOU'VE BEEN HEARD.
THE PROBLEM ISN'T OTHERS
KNOWING YOUR TONE OF VOICE, IS YOU!

LEARN YOUR LOVE LANGUAGE,
IN SPIRIT WITH WISDOM.
IF YOU CHOOSE NOT TO,

. . .
PLEASE NOTE
. . .

YOU'RE THAT BORED WITH YOURSELF!

Call Your POWER Back!

Manifest The Life You Don't Need A Vacation From:

Be ENCHANTING.
ENVISION What You See For Yourself.
VIBRATE With Gratitude.

_____

_____

_____

_____

_____

_____

_____

_____

_____

_____

_____

DATE: MANIFESTATION GOAL:

I'M GRATEFUL FOR: ONE STEP @ A TIME:

Manifest The Life You Don't Need A Vacation From:

CREATE YOUR HAPPINESS:

Be ENCHANTING.
ENVISION What You See For Yourself.
VIBRATE With Gratitude.

_____

_____

_____

_____

_____

_____

_____

_____

_____

_____

_____

_____

_____

_____

_____

_____

_____

_____

#JUSTMYTHOUGHTS

REASON

WHY I DON'T RUN AWAY FROM IT,

.,.

BECAUSE

I HAVE

ENOUGH

JOY

RUNNIN' TO IT.

IN PURPOSE

Surrender To Your Mission.

Manifest The Life You Don't Need A Vacation From:

Be ENCHANTING.
ENVISION What You See For Yourself.
VIBRATE With Gratitude.

_____

_____

_____

_____

_____

_____

_____

_____

_____

_____

_____

_____

DATE: MANIFESTATION GOAL:

I'M GRATEFUL FOR: ONE STEP @ A TIME:

Manifest The Life You Don't Need A Vacation From:

CREATE YOUR HAPPINESS:

Be ENCHANTING.
ENVISION What You See For Yourself.
VIBRATE With Gratitude.

_____

_____

_____

_____

_____

_____

_____

_____

_____

_____

_____

_____

_____

_____

_____

BIRTH.
DEATH.
LOVE.
EXPERIENCE.
&
ABUNDANCE.

-

#THINGSTHATWEREMEANT2GROWYOU

Trust The Process!

Manifest The Life You Don't Need A Vacation From:

Be ENCHANTING.
ENVISION What You See For Yourself.
VIBRATE With Gratitude.

_____

_____

_____

_____

_____

_____

_____

_____

_____

_____

_____

DATE: MANIFESTATION GOAL:

I'M GRATEFUL FOR: ONE STEP @ A TIME:

Manifest The Life You Don't Need A Vacation From:

CREATE YOUR HAPPINESS:

Be ENCHANTING.
ENVISION What You See For Yourself.
VIBRATE With Gratitude.

_____

_____

_____

_____

_____

_____

_____

_____

_____

_____

_____

_____

_____

_____

#JUSTMYTHOUGHTS

SO I GOTTA SPICE UP
MY HALLOWEEN COSTUME.
SHOULD I BE AS CREATIVE
AS THE UNNERVED
WHO SAY IT BOUT ME,
BUT NOT TO ME ?!

. . .

MAYBE I'LL BE:

. . .

- UGLY INSTEAD OF KNOWIN' MY WHOLE FAM IS GORGEOUS.
- A MOM OF 4 KIDS INSTEAD OF 1 LIVNG DAUGHTER & 1 DEAD SON.
- 2 FACED INSTEAD OF UNDERSTANDING, NON-JUDGEMENT & COURTEOUS.
- AT THE CLINIC CUZ OF SOMEONE I NEVER EXPERIENCED SEX WITH.
- A COKEHEAD, INSTEAD OF BEING SMOKE FREE 10YRS STRONG.
- FAT & SLOPPY INSTEAD OF AS THICK AS JIFFYS.
- STRETCHED IN A 3SOME INSTEAD OF DUDES LYING ON THEY EGGPLANT.
- FITTIN' IN INSTEAD OF KNOWIN' I WAS BORN TO STAND OUT.
- FOLK INSTEAD OF KNOWIN' MY CIRLE TIGHTER THAN A PERIOD.
- A STR8 ^ ASSHOLE INSTEAD OF THE HEART OF GOLD, YOU MISS!
- FUCK'N & FALL'N INSTEAD OF SINGLE & PLAYIN' W/...NEVERMIND!
- STUCK UP INSTEAD OF YOUR LAID BACK, FUN-LOVING & PEACEFUL.
- ON THAT "BUM SHIT" LYING, INSTEAD OF NOT GIVIN' A DAMN!

WELL,
HOW IMA TWERK THIS COSTUME ?!

. . .

OH! I GOT IT,
WITH MY
SONREÍR

Divine & Align.

Manifest The Life You Don't Need A Vacation From:

Be ENCHANTING.
ENVISION What You See For Yourself.
VIBRATE With Gratitude.

_____

_____

_____

_____

_____

_____

_____

_____

_____

_____

_____

_____

DATE: MANIFESTATION GOAL:

I'M GRATEFUL FOR: ONE STEP @ A TIME:

Manifest The Life You Don't Need A Vacation From:

CREATE YOUR HAPPINESS:

Be ENCHANTING.
ENVISION What You See For Yourself.
VIBRATE With Gratitude.

_____
_____
_____
_____
_____
_____
_____
_____
_____
_____
_____
_____
_____
_____
_____
_____
_____
_____
_____

EAT IT
ALL UP
-
FAST
OR
SLOW
-
WITHIN
FIVE MINS +
DO <u>NOT</u> LEAVE
A MESS BEHIND!

Take Action When Guided.

Manifest The Life You Don't Need A Vacation From:

Be ENCHANTING.
ENVISION What You See For Yourself.
VIBRATE With Gratitude.

_____

_____

_____

_____

_____

_____

_____

_____

_____

_____

_____

DATE: MANIFESTATION GOAL:

I'M GRATEFUL FOR: ONE STEP @ A TIME:

Manifest The Life You Don't Need A Vacation From:

Be ENCHANTING.
ENVISION What You See For Yourself.
VIBRATE With Gratitude.

_____

_____

_____

_____

_____

_____

_____

_____

_____

_____

_____

_____

_____

_____

_____

_____

#JUSTMYTHOUGHTS

"ASK"

AS YOU SHOULD
BEFORE YOU
"ASS"UME

—

NOTICE HOW
ASK ONLY
HAS 1 "S".

—

#ITBETHEHOLEY(1)S

TEND TO THE CRACKS
IN YOUR FOUNDATION
BEFORE YOU COME FOR ME.

Experience Is Wisdom.

Manifest The Life You Don't Need A Vacation From:

CREATE YOUR HAPPINESS:

Be ENCHANTING.
ENVISION What You See For Yourself.
VIBRATE With Gratitude.

_____

_____

_____

_____

_____

_____

_____

_____

_____

_____

_____

DATE: MANIFESTATION GOAL:

I'M GRATEFUL FOR: ONE STEP @ A TIME:

Manifest The Life You Don't Need A Vacation From:

CREATE YOUR HAPPINESS:

Be ENCHANTING.
ENVISION What You See For Yourself.
VIBRATE With Gratitude.

VERSATILE
IN
NATURE

AGILE
WITH
COMMUNICATION

#SelfCare Is A Must!

Manifest The Life You Don't Need A Vacation From:

CREATE YOUR HAPPINESS:

Be ENCHANTING.
ENVISION What You See For Yourself.
VIBRATE With Gratitude.

_____

_____

_____

_____

_____

_____

_____

_____

_____

_____

_____

DATE: MANIFESTATION GOAL:

I'M GRATEFUL FOR: ONE STEP @ A TIME:

Manifest The Life You Don't Need A Vacation From:

_____

_____

_____

_____

_____

_____

_____

_____

_____

_____

_____

_____

_____

_____

_____

_____

_____

#JUSTMYTHOUGHTS

PSSTTT!
THE PROBLEM COULD BE.

–

ALL THAT HOPE
MS. AMERICA SOLD YA'LL
.
.
.
.
.
.
.
.
.
.
IS
WEARING
OFF!

Ritual With Consistency!

Manifest The Life You Don't Need A Vacation From:

CREATE YOUR HAPPINESS:

Be ENCHANTING.
ENVISION What You See For Yourself.
VIBRATE With Gratitude.

_____

_____

_____

_____

_____

_____

_____

_____

_____

_____

_____

_____

DATE: MANIFESTATION GOAL:

I'M GRATEFUL FOR: ONE STEP @ A TIME:

Manifest The Life You Don't Need A Vacation From:

CREATE YOUR HAPPINESS:

Be ENCHANTING.
ENVISION What You See For Yourself.
VIBRATE With Gratitude.

_____

_____

_____

_____

_____

_____

_____

_____

_____

_____

_____

_____

_____

_____

_____

_____

YOU CAN'T
USE IT
AS A WAY TO
"CONVINCE" HER,
CUZ SHE
WAS NEVER
IN LOVE
WITH
THE
DICK!

.

.

DUMMY

.

.

Call Your POWER Back!

Manifest The Life You Don't Need A Vacation From:

CREATE YOUR HAPPINESS:

Be ENCHANTING.
ENVISION What You See For Yourself.
VIBRATE With Gratitude.

_____

_____

_____

_____

_____

_____

_____

_____

_____

_____

DATE: MANIFESTATION GOAL:

I'M GRATEFUL FOR: ONE STEP @ A TIME:

Manifest The Life You Don't Need A Vacation From:

CREATE YOUR HAPPINESS:

Be ENCHANTING.
ENVISION What You See For Yourself.
VIBRATE With Gratitude.

_____

_____

_____

_____

_____

_____

_____

_____

_____

_____

_____

_____

_____

_____

_____

_____

_____

_____

#JUSTMYTHOUGHTS

I PROMISE THERE IS
A TIME & PLACE
FOR EVERYTHING
SO IF NOT NOW

.,.
CRY
ABOUT IT
LATER!

#MOVEWITHPURPOSE

Surrender To Your Mission.

Manifest The Life You Don't Need A Vacation From:

Be ENCHANTING.
ENVISION What You See For Yourself.
VIBRATE With Gratitude.

_____

_____

_____

_____

_____

_____

_____

_____

_____

_____

_____

_____

_____

DATE: MANIFESTATION GOAL:

I'M GRATEFUL FOR: ONE STEP @ A TIME:

Manifest The Life You Don't Need A Vacation From:

CREATE YOUR HAPPINESS:

Be ENCHANTING.
ENVISION What You See For Yourself.
VIBRATE With Gratitude.

_____

_____

_____

_____

_____

_____

_____

_____

_____

_____

_____

_____

_____

_____

_____

_____

_____

_____

IT'S FUNNY
HOW YOU THINK
YOU KNOW MY STORY,
WHEN I'M NOT
DONE WRITING.
-
I'M JUST GETTING
TO THE PROLOGUE.

#JACKOFFJILL

. . . .

Trust The Process!

Manifest The Life You Don't Need A Vacation From:

CREATE YOUR HAPPINESS:

Be ENCHANTING.
ENVISION What You See For Yourself.
VIBRATE With Gratitude.

_____

_____

_____

_____

_____

_____

_____

_____

_____

_____

_____

_____

DATE: MANIFESTATION GOAL:

I'M GRATEFUL FOR: ONE STEP @ A TIME:

Manifest The Life You Don't Need A Vacation From:

CREATE YOUR HAPPINESS:

Be ENCHANTING.
ENVISION What You See For Yourself.
VIBRATE With Gratitude.

_____

_____

_____

_____

_____

_____

_____

_____

_____

_____

_____

_____

_____

_____

_____

#JUSTMYTHOUGHTS

JUST BCUZ
YOU TELL ME
SHIT I MAY
WANT TO HEAR
DOESN'T MEAN
I'M LISTENING
-_-
HOWEVER,
I'M ALWAYS
PAYING
ATTENTION!

Divine & Align.

Manifest The Life You Don't Need A Vacation From:

Be ENCHANTING.
ENVISION What You See For Yourself.
VIBRATE With Gratitude.

_____

_____

_____

_____

_____

_____

_____

_____

_____

_____

_____

_____

DATE: MANIFESTATION GOAL:

I'M GRATEFUL FOR: ONE STEP @ A TIME:

Manifest The Life You Don't Need A Vacation From:

Be ENCHANTING.
ENVISION What You See For Yourself.
VIBRATE With Gratitude.

_____

_____

_____

_____

_____

_____

_____

_____

_____

_____

_____

_____

_____

_____

_____

_____

_____

TRUST THAT
THE ONES
YOU CHOOSE
TO HOLD
DOWN,
WILL DO
THE SAME
FOR YOU
IF THE
SITUATION
SHIFTED
'ROUND!

Take Action When Guided.

Manifest The Life You Don't Need A Vacation From:

CREATE YOUR HAPPINESS:

Be ENCHANTING.
ENVISION What You See For Yourself.
VIBRATE With Gratitude.

_____

_____

_____

_____

_____

_____

_____

_____

_____

_____

_____

DATE: MANIFESTATION GOAL:

I'M GRATEFUL FOR: ONE STEP @ A TIME:

Manifest The Life You Don't Need A Vacation From:

Be ENCHANTING.
ENVISION What You See For Yourself.
VIBRATE With Gratitude.

_____

_____

_____

_____

_____

_____

_____

_____

_____

_____

_____

_____

_____

_____

_____

_____

#JUSTMYTHOUGHTS

SHOUTOUT TO
EVERY GOD-ESSENCE
NURTURING MOTHER READING:

I SALUTE YOU FOR BE-ING A WOMAN.
NOT IGNORANT, PREDICTABLE & SIMPLE-MINDED.

I SALUTE YOU FOR BE-ING A NURTURING MOTHER.
NOT JUST SOMEBODY'S "BABY MAMA".

I SALUTE YOU FOR RAISING YOUR KIDS YOUR WAY.
NOT USING THEM AS A PAYCHECK.

I SALUTE YOU FOR OWNING YOUR MIND & BODY.
NOT ALLOWING A NIGGA TO WALTZ OVER YOU.

I SALUTE YOU ACQUIRING THIRST IN KNOWLEDGE.
NOT THIRSTING FOR ATTENTION.

I SALUTE YOU AS ARE.
I SALUTE YOU IN YOUR RIGHT ACTION.
I SALUTE YOUR WORDS OF POWER.

SO TO YOU A TRUE GOD-ESSESNCE
THIS IS DEDICATED TO YOU!

#RESPECT
YOU WERE BORN AS IT!

Experience Is Wisdom.

Manifest The Life You Don't Need A Vacation From:

CREATE YOUR HAPPINESS:

Be ENCHANTING.
ENVISION What You See For Yourself.
VIBRATE With Gratitude.

_____

_____

_____

_____

_____

_____

_____

_____

_____

_____

_____

DATE: MANIFESTATION GOAL:

I'M GRATEFUL FOR: ONE STEP @ A TIME:

Manifest The Life You Don't Need A Vacation From:

CREATE YOUR HAPPINESS:

Be ENCHANTING.
ENVISION What You See For Yourself.
VIBRATE With Gratitude.

_____

_____

_____

_____

_____

_____

_____

_____

_____

_____

_____

_____

_____

_____

_____

_____

#JUSTMYTHOUGHTS

TRUTH IS IF I COULD CHOOSE ANYONE

...

IT WOULD STILL BE YOU!

#SelfCare Is A Must!

Manifest The Life You Don't Need A Vacation From:

CREATE YOUR HAPPINESS:

Be ENCHANTING.
ENVISION What You See For Yourself.
VIBRATE With Gratitude.

_____

_____

_____

_____

_____

_____

_____

_____

_____

_____

_____

_____

DATE: MANIFESTATION GOAL:

I'M GRATEFUL FOR: ONE STEP @ A TIME:

Manifest The Life You Don't Need A Vacation From:

CREATE YOUR HAPPINESS:

Be ENCHANTING.
ENVISION What You See For Yourself.
VIBRATE With Gratitude.

#JUSTMYTHOUGHTS

I JUST BE
CREATING PEACE,
FEELIN' MYSELF!

-

CARE TO JOIN IN?!

-

?NAH NEVERMIND¿

-

YOU PROLLY WON'T
RUB ME THE
RIGHT WAY

-

ANYWHO

Ritual With Consistency!

Manifest The Life You Don't Need A Vacation From:

Be ENCHANTING.
ENVISION What You See For Yourself.
VIBRATE With Gratitude.

_____

_____

_____

_____

_____

_____

_____

_____

_____

_____

_____

_____

_____

DATE: MANIFESTATION GOAL:

I'M GRATEFUL FOR: ONE STEP @ A TIME:

Manifest The Life You Don't Need A Vacation From:

Be ENCHANTING.
ENVISION What You See For Yourself.
VIBRATE With Gratitude.

_____

_____

_____

_____

_____

_____

_____

_____

_____

_____

_____

_____

_____

_____

_____

_____

WHEN
I WAS 14
MY HYMEN
WAS STILL
IN TACT

. . .

UNTIL
CHRISTMAS
CAME AROUND
THAT YEAR.

I WAS IN
LOVE & BROKE.

-_-

Call Your POWER Back!

Manifest The Life You Don't Need A Vacation From:

Be ENCHANTING.
ENVISION What You See For Yourself.
VIBRATE With Gratitude.

_____

_____

_____

_____

_____

_____

_____

_____

_____

_____

_____

DATE: MANIFESTATION GOAL:

I'M GRATEFUL FOR: ONE STEP @ A TIME:

Manifest The Life You Don't Need A Vacation From:

CREATE YOUR HAPPINESS:

Be ENCHANTING.
ENVISION What You See For Yourself.
VIBRATE With Gratitude.

#JUSTMYTHOUGHTS

I BELIEVE
THE SUN
HAS RISEN
NOT BECAUSE
OF IT'S GLOW

~ YET ~

EVERYTHING
EYE SEE
BY WAY OF
THE LIGHT.

#RISEANDBEGRAND

Surrender To Your Mission.

Manifest The Life You Don't Need A Vacation From:

CREATE YOUR HAPPINESS:

Be ENCHANTING.
ENVISION What You See For Yourself.
VIBRATE With Gratitude.

_____

_____

_____

_____

_____

_____

_____

_____

_____

_____

_____

DATE: MANIFESTATION GOAL:

I'M GRATEFUL FOR: ONE STEP @ A TIME:

Manifest The Life You Don't Need A Vacation From:

CREATE YOUR HAPPINESS:

Be ENCHANTING.
ENVISION What You See For Yourself.
VIBRATE With Gratitude.

_____

_____

_____

_____

_____

_____

_____

_____

_____

_____

_____

_____

_____

_____

_____

_____

_____

#JUSTMYTHOUGHTS

IF THAT'S
WHAT YOU THINK,
BY ALL MEANS;
THINK DAT!

—

IF THAT'S
WHAT YOU KNOW,
BY ALL MEANS;
KNOW THAT!

—

IF THAT'S
WHAT YOU BELIEVE,
BY ALL MEANS;
TRUST THAT!

—

IF THAT'S
HOW YOU LIVIN,
BY ALL MEANS;
LIVE BY THAT!

Trust The Process!

Manifest The Life You Don't Need A Vacation From:

CREATE YOUR HAPPINESS:

Be ENCHANTING.
ENVISION What You See For Yourself.
VIBRATE With Gratitude.

_____

_____

_____

_____

_____

_____

_____

_____

_____

_____

_____

DATE: MANIFESTATION GOAL:

I'M GRATEFUL FOR: ONE STEP @ A TIME:

Manifest The Life You Don't Need A Vacation From:

#JUSTMYTHOUGHTS

FAMILY, FOE,
LOVER OR FRIEND
THIS IS A REMINDER:
ONLY A FEW PPL CARE!
–

THE REST ARE JUST CURIOUS,
NOSEY BOOGERS ;P
PLACE YOUR FAITH
WHERE GENUINE LOVE IS.
REGARDLESS OF
WHOEVER, WHEREVER,
HOWEVER & WHATEVER
. . .
IT'LL STILL BE THERE,
WHETHER YOU WANT IT
OR NOT & FOR SURE
ALWAYS WHEN YOU NEED IT!
–

& UNLESS YOU CAN MATCH THAT
WITHOUT A "SHADOW" OF DOUBT
. . .
YOU'RE NOT REQUIRED TO
OWE ANYBODY, ANYTHING!

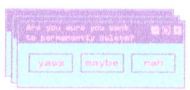

Divine & Align.

Manifest The Life You Don't Need A Vacation From:

_____

_____

_____

_____

_____

_____

_____

_____

_____

_____

DATE: MANIFESTATION GOAL:

I'M GRATEFUL FOR: ONE STEP @ A TIME:

Manifest The Life You Don't Need A Vacation From:

CREATE YOUR HAPPINESS:

Be ENCHANTING.
ENVISION What You See For Yourself.
VIBRATE With Gratitude.

_____

_____

_____

_____

_____

_____

_____

_____

_____

_____

_____

_____

_____

_____

_____

_____

_____

I NEED

TO SEE

YOU SAYIN'

THE SAME THING

I FEEL, WITHOUT

YOUR LIPS MOVING

& ALL THAT BACK TALK

 . . . .

Take Action When Guided.

Manifest The Life You Don't Need A Vacation From:

CREATE YOUR HAPPINESS:

Be ENCHANTING.
ENVISION What You See For Yourself.
VIBRATE With Gratitude.

_____

_____

_____

_____

_____

_____

_____

_____

_____

_____

DATE: MANIFESTATION GOAL:

I'M GRATEFUL FOR: ONE STEP @ A TIME:

Manifest The Life You Don't Need A Vacation From:

CREATE YOUR HAPPINESS:

Be ENCHANTING.
ENVISION What You See For Yourself.
VIBRATE With Gratitude.

_____

_____

_____

_____

_____

_____

_____

_____

_____

_____

_____

_____

_____

_____

_____

_____

_____

#JUSTMYTHOUGHTS

LADIES:
MEN ARE NOT
"HEARTLESS, BASTARDS,
DICKHEADS, CHEATERS,
LIARS & ASSHOLES"

-THOSE ARE THEM LIL' BOYS-

GIVE THE MEN
SOME CREDIT
-_-
"WHEN"
YOU COME ACROSS ONE
. . . .

Experience Is Wisdom.

Manifest The Life You Don't Need A Vacation From:

CREATE YOUR HAPPINESS:

Be ENCHANTING.
ENVISION What You See For Yourself.
VIBRATE With Gratitude.

_____

_____

_____

_____

_____

_____

_____

_____

_____

_____

_____

_____

DATE: MANIFESTATION GOAL:

I'M GRATEFUL FOR: ONE STEP @ A TIME:

Manifest The Life You Don't Need A Vacation From:

CREATE YOUR HAPPINESS:

Be ENCHANTING.
ENVISION What You See For Yourself.
VIBRATE With Gratitude.

_____

_____

_____

_____

_____

_____

_____

_____

_____

_____

_____

_____

_____

_____

_____

_____

_____

#JUSTMYTHOUGHTS

WHY BEG
FOR SOMETHING
FROM SOMEONE ELSE
THAT YOU CAN
GIVE YOURSELF?!
-

I NEED YOU

TO POUR INTO ME
NOT DRAIN
WHAT'S
LEFT
OUT
OF
ME
.
.
.

#SelfCare Is A Must!

Manifest The Life You Don't Need A Vacation From:

_____

_____

_____

_____

_____

_____

_____

_____

_____

_____

DATE: MANIFESTATION GOAL:

I'M GRATEFUL FOR: ONE STEP @ A TIME:

Manifest The Life You Don't Need A Vacation From:

CREATE YOUR HAPPINESS:

Be ENCHANTING.
ENVISION What You See For Yourself.
VIBRATE With Gratitude.

_____

_____

_____

_____

_____

_____

_____

_____

_____

_____

_____

_____

_____

_____

_____

#JUSTMYTHOUGHTS

YOU
GOTTA BE WATCHFUL.
GOTTA BE GRATEFUL.
GOTTA BE FAITHFUL.
GOTTA BE THANKFUL.
BE INTENTIONAL.
AND
BE PURPOSEFUL.
-
IN SPIRIT AS WELL AS
IN YOUR WORDS OF POWER
AS YOU RECEIVE
DIVINE BLESSINGS!

Ritual With Consistency!